LIFE ON THE PORCH

From Comfort to Connection with God

Jim Vernon

Reach... Grow... DO

Contents

Introduction   5

1: Hanging Out on the Porch   11
2: Lukewarm   20
3: 2006: A Vernon Odyssey   28
4: Inside   46
5: My Own Walk to Emmaus   53
6: Keep on Keeping On   61
7: Not All Rainbows and Unicorns   69
8: Send in the Cavalry, I Need Calvary!   77

Now What?   81

Introduction

It's all about the story, and everyone has one. Some people have extraordinary tales about their lives or careers, and some people have stories that may seem mundane or routine. Some people like talking or writing about themselves, and some people are much more private about their lives. Although I've never been very comfortable talking about myself, I have felt compelled to share this particular story of my faith, my family, and our journey through cancer.

A few years ago a friend of mine, knowing some details of what my family had been through, asked me to share my story with his Sunday school class. The first question I asked myself was, "What exactly *is* my story?" I assumed that since I would be speaking to a Sunday school class, I should talk about the role God has played in my life. When I started to think about what I would say, the topics of faith, cancer, and my life as viewed from the front porch seemed to feel like a testimony, which I had never thought about before.

I grew up in a small town in Kentucky, but have had the opportunity to see most of the United States, and even travel abroad some. I have a younger sister, and we grew up in a loving home, despite the fact that our parents divorced while we were both in college. As of this writing, I've been married for twenty-six years and have two beautiful daughters. I feel like I've lived an interesting life, but I never thought my story was all that remarkable. However, somewhere along the line, I had shared enough about my life that I was asked to do it in a more formal way—in front of a group of real, live people! What was I going to say?

My pastor says that we are all part of the Great Story. I believe that, but I wasn't always convinced my part of it was anything people would care about hearing. I told myself that there was nothing special about my story, and I didn't see how it could be impactful for anyone. The problem was that I kept having this nagging feeling that I was supposed to "do" something with it. There wasn't a specific "aha" moment, but it seemed like things kept happening that made me think about what I should do with my story, such as comments from friends or sermons that stirred up memories. So I prayed for wisdom and guidance.

In the fall of 2012, two weeks before I was invited to talk in that Sunday school class, I asked God for some direction on what I should share. I knew basically what I wanted to say, but I had never organized my thoughts in a way to present it as a talk. I made notes in case I went completely blank, but when it came time to speak, I wasn't terribly nervous and it went well. I talked for nearly a half hour and received some good feedback when I was finished. In fact, I noticed one lady tearing up while I was speaking, so I knew I had made some kind of impact.

A couple of months later, I was asked to speak again at a local civic club. One of my customers at work knew a little about my personal life, and he said he felt like I had a story that would fit well with his group.

Several months later, I decided to tell my pastor about my feelings. I had now shared my story twice publicly, and I could tell it was resonating with people. My wife has consistently told me to share this story in any way I could. Still, I kept arguing with myself despite what I was feeling. I don't know how else to describe it other than I felt as though I was being pushed. I've often heard people say that God "nudged" them to do things, but this was past nudging.

I planned on talking to my pastor before the service one Sunday, but he was extra busy, so I decided to wait until after the service. My jaw dropped when he challenged us all that morning to consider sharing our stories with the congregation. I knew it was a sign and an answer.

I gave my testimony in church on Mother's Day 2015 to around 150 congregants, and although I was nervous, it was well received. I had now shared some version of the same story three times publically, and more people were starting to respond. Common responses were "I have the same feelings" and "I can really relate" from both friends and strangers. It seemed like I was supposed to keep doing it.

I felt like God was leading me, but I was worried this was more about me than about God. Many times throughout this process, I've struggled with whether to write my story because I was afraid it might be more about my own pride or ego. I'm not a big fan of people who feel the need to draw attention to themselves. In life, business, sports, or whatever, I'm always drawn to those who are successful but don't need to talk about it. But like I said, the feeling wouldn't go away. In fact, it was getting stronger.

At some point between my first two talks and that Mother's Day testimony, I experienced something of a tipping point. I had been praying for some guidance on how or if to share this story more, and during a flight one morning, I happened to look over the shoulder of a man reading a blog concerning this very subject. I got nosy and started reading the article too, and a line stood out to me that said something like: "Put away your false humility and do what you feel like you are supposed to do for God."

So after all of those signs and feelings, I finally said, "Okay, Lord, I get it." So, here I go . . .

1

Hanging Out on the Porch

For the better part of my adult life, I have described my spiritual life as though I was outside of a house on the front porch looking inside at what a *real* relationship with God was like. The issue for me was that for some reason I wouldn't go inside. I thought there had to be another level of feeling I was missing. Too many things seemed routine or too ritualized for what I thought *real* meant. I don't know why I wouldn't go on in. Maybe I thought it was going to be weird inside. Maybe I didn't think I would fit in. Maybe I didn't think I was good enough. I think a lot of it was being comfortable on the porch. I had a comfortable routine. I had gotten used to how life was and what my role was. I knew what everything was like on the porch. I knew what was expected of me—and *not* expected of me—on the porch. I had heard that it was nice inside, but it was unknown and unpredictable.

I was probably like a lot of people who are kind of cruising along through life. I believed in God. I felt like I was a generally "good" person. I tried to be kind to others. I didn't feel much of a need to make more of an impact around me. If the opportunity to do more slapped me in the face, I might do it, but I didn't have much initiative. As I grew into my late thirties, the question in my mind became, "Is this it?" I knew that there had to be more to God, me, life, and what it's all supposed to be about. I wanted a deeper awareness of something more significant than I had ever felt.

I continued to have these fleeting feelings, but didn't know what to do with them. And to do anything would have required getting out of my comfort zone. Isn't it amazing what we will do—or *not* do—to be comfortable in every part of our lives? I didn't even realize I was on the "porch," or there was an "inside." It's only when I look back that I can make this analogy.

In fact, John Wesley (founder of the Methodist Church) used the analogy of a house when he described his ideas on the three types of grace. He actually used the porch of the house to describe prevenient grace—God actively seeking a relationship with us before we know it. The door of the house represents justifying grace—an assurance we receive when we walk through it that all our sins are forgiven. And finally, sanctifying grace is the interior of the house, where we mature in our faith. I had never heard or read that when I started using the porch analogy. I only realized it a few years later as I was reading about Wesley.

While I was preparing a talk for my Sunday school class, I needed some information on prevenient grace. When I started reading about Wesley's house analogy, my first thought was, *Well, that's it. I'm not the first one to think of this whole "porch" thing. I might as well stop telling my story!* But I figured there had to be a reason I felt compelled to share, so I decided to give Wesley his due and keep on going. I was really bummed at first that I didn't have a completely original thought, but at least I knew it wasn't a crazy thought.

I developed my analogy after hearing a brief part of a country song years ago called "My Front Porch Looking In." The lyrics describe looking in the house from the front porch at what is really important. Now, anyone who knows me will chuckle at the notion that I got some type of thought or idea from a country song. No disrespect, but it's a genre that doesn't appeal to me. I didn't even know who sang the song until I was writing this testimony. God *really* must have been trying to talk to me, but I just couldn't hear it yet. I wasn't ready to get uncomfortable. I think my faith had been on cruise control for so long that I wasn't used to really driving. God was telling me to get rid of the nice sedan that shifts gears so smoothly and start driving a stick shift, but I continued to hesitate.

I've thought a lot about the comfort of being on the porch and how it kept me from going inside. Most of my life—or at least adult life—I didn't consider what faith really meant, looked like, or felt like. If you're picturing the "porch" in your life, I'm sure you have a particular image in mind. I picture my porch to be part of a cabin that looks very much like the one my mother and stepfather built on some farmland in middle Tennessee while my wife and I were expecting our first child almost two decades ago. There are no other houses in sight, and it's surrounded by beautiful hills, trees, and farmland. Yours may be part of any type of house or structure, in any part of the world. In my analogy, the porch is a place that's just on the periphery of what I call the "real stuff."

The porch is a nice place to hang out. Mine's got a couple of comfortable rocking chairs, a swing, and something to put your feet up on if you want. The furniture is soft and comfortable. There is plenty of shade, and somehow the temperature is always just right. It's easy to want to stay there all the time. There are plenty of windows on the front of the cabin, so I have lots of opportunities to see inside. It's unclear what's going on in there, but I have the distinct feeling it's important and meaningful. I just can't see it clearly while I'm standing outside. Besides, I tell myself there is enough activity on the porch to have a fulfilling life. Family, job, sports, hobbies, entertainment—all become part of life on the porch. If I have time, I may squeeze God into that routine. Things aren't always perfect on the porch, but it's a comfortable place to be as life goes on. I don't mean to suggest that many of the things on the porch are not significant. I am suggesting that all of those things kept me busy enough to never really consider there was something more.

I spent much of my life content being on the porch and looking out toward the yard, away from the house. Think Andy and Barney from the old *Andy Griffith Show*—when they were in black and white, of course. It was never the same after Barney left and they were in color—but I digress. If you're old enough, are you picturing the look of contentment on their faces while they sit on Andy's front porch? People stop by for small talk, or just to check in with one another. So it was on my porch. People came and went. Some stayed longer than others, depending on how they fit into my life. A whole lot of life happened outside . . . it still does. And I consider myself fortunate to have had such a life on that porch.

As I got older and had children, however, I started to look over my shoulder to see what was going on inside. I had no particular image when I looked in there. It was more of a feeling - a feeling that I needed to know what it would be like if I stepped over that threshold. Speaking of the doorway, I don't recall thinking about it or picturing it in my mind. Whatever it was, I knew it wouldn't be hard to open; I just had to do it. Yet I continued to hesitate, even though I couldn't help but wonder if I was missing something by not going inside. I knew I was going to be uncomfortable to take the step, but I didn't know why.

Eventually it started to occur to me that striving for comfort in our lives is not what it's all about. When we are comfortable, there doesn't seem to be a reason to reach for anything more or different. It all too often makes us sedentary and less likely to challenge ourselves. It can make us feel safe and sometimes oblivious to things.

This is not an easy thing to realize in society today—particularly American society. Every time you turn around, the word *comfort* is used as a goal to be attained: a comfortable lifestyle, a comfortable job, comfortable retirement . . . I don't think there is anything inherently wrong with being comfortable, unless that becomes the grand prize. I know I'm painting with a broad brush here, and you may say you see no reason or purpose to leave the comfort of your porch. I'm talking about being *too* comfortable—so comfortable that we start coasting through our spiritual walk. At that time, God and faith were part of my life—just not a meaningful part of my life. The key word in that last sentence is *meaningful.* I went to church and prayed every so often, but I'm not sure there was much substance in what I was doing—and there sure wasn't much feeling. My spiritual walk had become way more walk than spirit.

We tell ourselves it's just the routine of a busy life, but really we don't feel anything deep down inside. We may not be able to put a finger on what that connection with God is supposed to feel like, but we know something is missing. The question becomes: Is life on the porch keeping us from moving forward in our lives—from seeking a real relationship with God and finding out what He wants us to do in this world, and doing it?

My comfort on the porch—and the general feeling I was a somewhat decent human—kept me on the fringe of the "real stuff." So there I was, staring inside, wondering.

2

Lukewarm

The way I heard it growing up was almost opposite from the way I felt. I was told you were inside your house, and Jesus was always on your doorstep. All you had to do was let Him in the door and into your life. I think that's true, but I've been a believer as long as I can remember. I let Him in a long time ago; I just never really got to know Him. Kind of like keeping Jesus in the mother-in-law suite.

I don't have a lightning-strike or mountain-top conversion experience to share. I wish I did. It would certainly be more interesting to talk or write about, and surely more interesting to hear or read about. I'm almost envious of those people who can name the time and place they were saved—particularly those who have fascinating stories or unusual circumstances. My road seemed to be gradual and more of a process—not exactly the kind of story that gets people fired up.

I grew up in a Methodist church. We didn't attend what I would call regularly—it was kind of streaky. We might go for three or four weeks in a row, and then not go for several weeks. I can't say I got much out of it, and usually I just felt like I was supposed to go. If we missed a lot, I might even feel a little guilty. We went because my mother said we were going, so I never questioned it much. But she had grown up in a much more strict tradition and had grown tired of the fire and brimstone she was accustomed to hearing about. However, even though we weren't regular attendees, I knew God was important to her.

At that time in his life, my father was indifferent toward God, but might go with us every now and then. I remember a few summers participating in vacation Bible school and several times my mother had to drag me to youth group. I knew most of the other kids a little bit, but wasn't there enough to create any lasting relationships. In a very general way I believed, but I never really thought that much about God. My life was filled with school, family, friends, and being on a basketball court or a golf course. God just barely made the top-ten list for me.

I went to Vanderbilt on a golf scholarship in 1983 and spent all my time playing golf, studying, partying, and sleeping—in no particular order. I didn't go to church a single time while I was at school. I went with my family some over the summers, but it made no real impression on me. I can't even recall many meaningful conversations about God growing up.

I married my wife, Beth, when I was twenty-four. She is a year younger than I am, and we had gone to school together since I was in the fifth grade. Interestingly enough, we never had a date throughout those school years. When we tell people we went to school together, they assume we were high school sweethearts, but it couldn't be further from the truth. In fact, we sat beside each other in a class one year and she hardly talked to me. We knew each other enough to be friendly, but didn't run in the same circles and never had much interaction.

The summer before my senior year in college, we ran into each other at a party and immediately clicked. Our summer fling turned into something much more serious. We married three and a half years later. The ceremony was in a church, mainly because that's what we thought you were supposed to do. I don't recall any specific conversations we had back then about God or faith. Beth had a similar church upbringing to mine, and I would say we had similar thoughts and feelings about God and church. I'm really only guessing we did because that's how little we talked about it. If you had asked us, we would have said we were Christians, but there was little substance. We attended when it was convenient, or maybe if we hadn't stayed out too late on Saturday night. We believed, but God was not an important part of our lives.

We were married eight years before we had children. After our second daughter was born, we decided we wanted them to grow up in the church. We had visited a Methodist church in our community several times over those eight years, and it seemed like a logical place to go, even though we really didn't know anyone very well. I don't remember what brought up the conversation, but we both thought it was a good idea. I look back now and think that was one of those prevenient grace moments. What would make a couple who paid little attention to God decide it was now important for their family? I don't know. I do know we attended church more regularly; we began to enjoy it more, and felt like we were learning, helping people, and increasing our faith. For the first time in our lives, we began to consider God as a regular part of our lives. But guess what? I was still hanging out on the porch, and I maintained my spot in my comfy rocker for the next two or three years.

Several years ago, I listened to a sermon about "lukewarm Christians." You may have experienced this, but it was one of those sermons that I was pretty sure was just for me. Everyone else could go on home because those words were meant for my ears only. I listened intently that day, and it really hit me hard. We went home and I said to my wife, "That sermon was for me. I *am* the definition of a lukewarm Christian. I believe, but there is absolutely nothing on fire inside me for the Lord." She looked at me and said, "You're right. What are we going to do?" After some thought I replied, "I have no idea. What *are* we going to do?"

We discussed it for a while and spanned the spectrum from selling all our stuff and being missionaries to helping old people cross the street. The kids were young and had already started school, so completely uprooting and changing our lives was out of the question. We decided the first step we would take would be to get more involved in our church, and let it help lead us with programs, missions, or initiatives.

Once again, I felt like we were doing some good, increasing our faith, and putting that faith into action. Even with all the positive things going on, I still would not walk on in off the porch. Something was holding me back, but I didn't know what it was. It's hard to explain what I thought was missing. I didn't even know what I was being held back from. It was a sense there was supposed to be something more to experience. What did a real relationship with God look like? I certainly didn't know.

Was there more to this relationship than just believing? Was I supposed to "do" something? If so, what? I can now see times that I was being pulled toward Him. I remember a specific instance when I was visiting my mother and we went to her church that Sunday. My wife and children were there with me, and it was a beautiful service. My stepfather plays the organ for the church, and it's one of the main reasons we love to go. I don't recall what the sermon was about, but at some point I got very emotional and started to feel warm all over. I'm not even sure it was the content of the sermon that touched me. You would think I would remember a message that sparked the feeling I've described, but I don't. I felt like I might cry and had no idea why. I considered getting up and leaving, but instead composed myself because I thought that's what I was supposed to do. I *knew* something was going on inside me . . . in my gut, or soul, or whatever it is. I either resisted it or didn't recognize it. Wesley described a "strange warming of the heart," but I just kept telling myself the air conditioning wasn't working as well as it should. Whatever the case, I stayed on my imaginary porch.

3

2006: A Vernon Odyssey

Most of 2006 is still like a bad dream to me, but it was also a defining year in my life. In May of that year—just shy of turning forty—Beth found a lump in her right breast while she was in the shower. Her doctor ordered an ultrasound and subsequent biopsy. We were nervous, but one of our nurses told us the majority of these things weren't cancer; plus, we had no history of cancer on either side of our families. We left the office feeling a little better than we did when we went in.

It's an image that still haunts me and I can never get completely out of my head: my then-five-year-old Anna running to me in the yard while I was mowing. It had been four or five days since the biopsy, and I had the day off from work. It was Tuesday, May 23. I'll never forget that day. Anna was yelling and crying, and I couldn't make out what she was saying. I turned off the mower to hear her shouting, "Daddy, there's something bad wrong with Mommy!" She had heard Beth on the answering machine trying to tell me through her tears that it was cancer. I hadn't had my cell phone on me since I was mowing. Beth had been sitting at her desk at work and the surgeon called and very matter-of-factly told her the news. He said we needed to come by the office sometime that afternoon to discuss what was next.

I left Anna with a friend and jumped in the car. Bailey, our eight-year-old, was still at school. I don't remember my specific thoughts, but I couldn't get to Beth fast enough. I found her slumped over in her car in the parking lot of her office building. There was something awful about sitting in that parking lot, so I put her in my car and we went up the street to a park. We got out and sat by one of the ponds just staring and crying.

Once we got it together, we started the process of figuring out how to proceed. My boss's wife had been through the same thing ten years earlier so we called them that afternoon for advice on navigating all that lay ahead of us. Their love and support was, and still is, something we knew we could count on. The meeting with the surgeon left us with as many questions as answers: Should they remove both breasts? Were lymph nodes involved? Was it anywhere else in her body? Surgery and a subsequent scan would give us much of the information we needed, so we scheduled them as soon as possible.

After countless doctors, appointments, and meetings, Beth had a double mastectomy exactly one month after that awful phone call. I was called into a little waiting room after the surgery to talk to the surgeon. I was all alone, and the only thing I can remember about the room was that it had a small crucifix hanging on the wall. I stared a hole through it and prayed for no lymph node involvement. The doctor walked in and told me there probably was node involvement and she had removed nineteen. We went home and prayed for limited node involvement, and the oncologist called two days later and said seventeen of the nineteen were cancerous. We prayed for her reconstruction surgery to be smooth, and she had complication after complication.

It seemed like every time we talked to a doctor, the worse the news became. That's when our friends started rallying around us. Beth's friends and our family gathered regularly with her to talk, listen, cry, laugh, and pray. Then I watched this amazing thing happen. She grew more confident and positive as time went on. I watched chemotherapy beat up her body, make her lose her hair, and cringe at the sight of her scars. After twelve weeks of radiation, the skin around her right breast looked like cooked bacon. Yet she still smiled every day and told me everything was going to be okay. *That was supposed to be my job!*

At first I was angry, but it seemed futile to be that way, and we were trying to be faithful and positive. I don't know if Beth's faith increased during that time, but she definitely had a peace about her that I didn't. Her strength and faith helped me.

As the weeks went on, and Beth went back to work, I got stronger, and the few times Beth had her low moments, I was able to be the husband and support I so wanted to be.

A few months went by. Beth's scans were still clear, and we felt like we were getting back to some sense of normalcy—or at least what we called "the new normal." By this time, Beth had finished her chemo and was getting ready to start radiation, so we took the kids to the beach in Destin, Florida, for a mini-vacation.

While we were driving, I felt a small knot on the back of my neck, not quite below my hairline. I've had several cysts cut out of my body over the years, so it shouldn't have been a big deal. Being a little hypersensitive to things at that point, I kept touching it repeatedly over those few days and had trouble getting it off my mind. I went to see my doctor when I got home and he guessed it was probably a cyst as well, but sent me down the hall to see a surgeon friend of his. The surgeon agreed and told me to watch it for any changes in size. I don't know if it changed in size, but I couldn't last a month, so I called him to take it out of me pronto. It was an easy procedure, and I would come back the following week to get my stitches out.

When I showed up the next week to have the stitches removed, my regular doctor was there waiting with the surgeon. I immediately knew something was wrong. He said, "I don't know how to tell you this, but what we took out is metastatic melanoma and we don't know where it started on your body." I instantly felt like I had been hit in the gut with a baseball bat. I was just getting my life back together after Beth's cancer!

They explained what might come next, and I knew it was very serious. More than likely, I would have more extensive surgery followed by a year of a drug that may or may not decrease my chances of it coming back. My doc, a friend of the family who knew what we had gone through, looked at me with sad eyes and said, "Don't be mad at God." I remember telling him I wasn't mad . . . I was going to need Him. I'm not sure why my first reaction wasn't to be angry, but I think going through this with Beth somehow prepared me for what I had to do, and it seemed a waste of time to be mad. The three of us prayed right there that I would have a good outcome. I went home and Googled *metastatic melanoma*, and that was a huge mistake. I quit reading after two minutes. It was ugly... really ugly.

I called Beth later that day as I picked up Bailey from day care. She couldn't wrap her head around it—nobody could at first. Everyone was in shock from the news. It didn't seem possible. It had only been six months since Beth's diagnosis, and the whirlwind started all over again. I called another pastor friend a few days later and told him what was up and that I really needed a prayer. His prayer began, "Lord . . . now come on! The Vernons have had enough!" It was the most real and appropriate prayer I could have ever prayed myself. That raw feeling was exactly what I needed.

I had another small surgery at the site on the back of my neck about two weeks later to clean up what was left. Then I was sent to have a full body

PET scan to see if there was any cancer in the rest of my body. Fortunately, my scan was clear, but I was quickly made aware that metastatic melanoma was a bad deal and there were very few options in treating it other than surgery. It was then determined that the most aggressive path for me would be to take out all the lymph nodes on the left side of my neck where it could most likely spread. So that's what I did.

I had a radical neck dissection and a three-inch incision on my head where a suspicious mole had been. With a ten-inch scar around my neck and a round bald spot on the side of my head, I looked like Frankenstein's monster for the next three months. I would then endure a year of a crappy drug called interferon that made me feel like I had the flu every day, but it also gave me an 8 to 10 percent better chance that the melanoma might not come back. Not great odds, but we felt like I should do everything possible to improve my chances. I got so used to feeling bad that I actually functioned pretty well.

We had to enlist help from family, friends, and co-workers to get through the next few months. Between both of our treatments, work, and two young children, we wouldn't have made it without a lot of help. Friends, family, and our church were unbelievable with their prayers and support. I also don't know how I would have made it without my work "family." Sometimes my boss took me to doctors' appointments because Beth and I had treatments or appointments on the same day. I had many sleepless nights from either anxiety or feeling sick, but I was able to use the model Beth had shown me to be positive, faithful, and ready to fight.

It was February of 2007, and Beth was on the back end of her radiation treatments when I started the interferon. The first month of that treatment required an infusion every day, Monday through Friday. After that, I would give myself a shot three days a week for the next eleven months. My mother came to help us that February with the kids and taking me to treatment since I couldn't drive home. After a couple of days, Mom decided that she would read to me during the infusion. Her material of choice was one of our favorites—David Sedaris. If you've ever read any of Sedaris's stuff, you know he is hilarious, serious, crude, and poignant, all rolled into one. There were many times we were laughing so loudly that the nurse would stick her head behind the curtain to see if we were doing okay. Mom would say, "Lord, there's got to be something wrong with laughing this hard with ten people all around us fighting for their lives." I hope it wasn't offensive to anyone else, because it helped me greatly. I finished that drug the following February, had another scan, and was told I would get another scan and checkup every six months going forward.

Between the two of us, we navigated the next five years pretty well, all things considered. Somehow we never found ourselves down or afraid at the same time. When she was down, I was able to be strong for her and vice versa.

I had what was supposed to be my last scan in the fall of 2011. All signs told my doctor that we could just go to six-month checkups and not have to scan so often. But that scan—just four months shy of five years after the initial diagnosis—showed a spot on my left lung. I had a pretty rough surgery to cut it out, and it was confirmed to be a melanoma recurrence. It was devastating news for everyone *again*. I had a clean scan ninety days after surgery, but the six-month scan showed another spot on the same lung. This news sent my thoughts spiraling out of control. I fought hard to keep my head up and remain positive.

I went to see my oncologist a couple of weeks after this latest scan and prepared myself for the "cut and hope/pray" speech, but he told me he was recommending me as a participant in a clinical trial involving a new immunotherapy drug that had showed promise in killing cells in several types of cancer, including melanoma. Everyone was nervous, but I was thankful to have another option than just surgery. The docs called the drug Anti PDL—PDL for short. My wife said PDL stood for

"Praise Da Lord." I started that trial in April of 2012.

I had an infusion every three weeks over the course of the next year and got used to staring at the white ceiling tiles at Vanderbilt Medical Center. At the first treatment, I was anxious and didn't feel like reading or watching TV. I had talked to my father a few days before, and he told me he had just finished the John Adams series on HBO. We're both movie buffs and like much of the same music, so he mentioned how great the soundtrack to the show was—particularly the opening theme. I remembered he called it "music for courage," so I found it on my phone and hit Play as the nurse started the infusion. I prayed to God to be healed and pictured that drug running throughout my body literally fighting anything that wasn't supposed to be there. That drug killed my tumor, and I had another lung surgery the following May to take out the remnants and confirm that the tissue was dead. I have been cancer-free ever since.

We never did spend much time in the "Why me?" frame of mind. The truth is, I said, "Why not me?" Yeah, it seemed really crappy and somewhat unbelievable that Beth and I had serious diagnoses that close together, at a pretty young age, while in good health. The truth is that terrible things happen all the time, and nobody is immune to that. I think that realization helped us both keep from feeling sorry for ourselves and keep moving forward. Plus, all you have to do is spend a little time in a cancer ward, and you know there is always someone worse off than you. Now, I do have to confess that sometimes we'll see some eighty-year-old, overweight person, with a cigarette and drink in their hand at ten o'clock in the morning and we'll say, "Really? And we got cancer?" In my "everything should be fair" mind, it doesn't seem like it ought to work that way, but I've realized that none of us are promised that this life will work out a certain way.

It's safe to say that Beth and I have had more doctor appointments, consultations, scans, surgeries, treatments, more surgeries, more treatments, more scans than I can count. Even though we're both cancer-free, it still goes on today, ten years later as of this writing. It's mostly checkups and scans now, but as Jason Robards says in the movie *Parenthood*, "You never really get to cross the goal line and spike the ball." We will always have to deal with it one way or another for the rest of our lives. Even though we decided early on that we would never be defined by cancer, it always has a way of working its way into things.

The second lung surgery left me with some new scars to add to my collection. Between the two of us, we look like pincushions. I was a few months post-surgery in 2013, and we were going out to dinner. We have two mirrors about four feet apart in our bathroom, and each of us was using one to get ready. As I looked at my reflection, I began to stare at all my battle marks, starting with my scalp and going down around my neck, chest, and back. I immediately put on a wounded kind of scowl. I glanced out of the corner of my eye at Beth, and she was doing the same thing to her body. She's had most everything removed that could be a potential recurrence spot. She had a similar look on her face, and we caught each other's glances. So we turned and faced each other in all our naked, middle-aged, battle-worn glory. There was silence for a few moments, and I expected one of us to say something really poignant or meaningful. Beth burst out with: "Whew! Honey! We are *really* bringing sexy back, aren't we!?" (And now I've worked Justin Timberlake and Andy Griffith into the same story. You're welcome). We laughed and cried at the same time. We do a lot of that at the Vernon house.

It's also safe to say that cancer has changed everyone's life in our family. My two daughters have had to deal with some pretty heady stuff at a young age. It has definitely given them a perspective that many kids their age don't have.

I'll never forget asking my oldest daughter Bailey's school counselor how she was doing when we were in the middle of our treatments. She told me Bailey said she didn't talk about it much at home, mainly because she knew we had enough to worry about without her adding to it. I cried like a baby knowing that my then-nine-year-old didn't want to seem like an additional burden to her own parents. *She* was thinking more about us than herself . . . at nine years old! Our youngest, Anna, was only five years old when Beth and I were diagnosed. She knew there was something serious happening, but wasn't quite sure what it all meant.

Thankfully, my mother has had success in talking with the girls about it. I recall a time when my mother was in town helping and she was putting Anna to bed and telling her a story. My mom asked if Anna would like to pray before they went to sleep and Anna agreed. Mom asked Anna if she liked to lie in bed and pray, or get down on her knees by the bed, or maybe pray by the window. Anna told her very plainly, "Granny, I think it's going to get to God no matter how we do it." I know Anna didn't understand the gravity of all that was happening, but there was a peace about her that was infectious in our family. I wish it had been something a whole lot easier than cancer, but I know it has made us all better human beings.

I don't like talking about cancer, and I don't write about it to call attention to what we've been through. I don't wear it like a badge of honor. It sucks. I'm sure I could write an entire book about our cancer journeys, but I am determined for this to be a God story and not a cancer story. I tell this part because the things we went through in 2006 made me walk on inside the house. *Cancer* made me walk on in off the porch.

For the longest time, I was ashamed to tell people that. Ashamed that I was so shallow to need something awful to make me look for more with God. I have since come to realize that for lots of people, it's those times when we are the most beaten down, depressed, afraid, or vulnerable that we are our most open to things. I have heard other people say this, but now I know it's really true.

There is a quote that is widely attributed to Abraham Lincoln during what I assume were some of the darkest days of his presidency. Referring to

God and prayer, he said, "I had nowhere else to go but my knees." That was me. I *wanted* to be more than just a believer. I *needed* to be more than just a believer. My insides *yearned* for it. So sometime in the summer of 2006, in the midst of cancer, I decided to walk on in . . .

4

Inside

Guess what? It's reeeaaallly nice inside. There is so much love and forgiveness. There is also a lot of responsibility inside, and that's okay with us. I have a responsibility to show my faith in a way that makes people want to come to God. The more we do, the more we *want* to do for God and others. The closer we get to God, the closer we *want* to get to God.

I even have an image of what it's like inside. I am completely surrounded by light. It's not that harsh white light you might see in an office building. It's a beautiful, warm, glowing light, and it's everywhere. I can't see anyone else, but I know there are other people in there—at least I think they are people. This image came from my mother when I asked her to pray for me before some of my treatments or when I was waiting on scan results. She would say, "Son, I'm holding you in God's light," and she would describe a beautiful light surrounding me.

I picture that cabin on the farm with light pouring out all the windows, and I see myself standing on the porch looking inside. My first view is from the road as I drive up to the cabin. I see a figure on the porch that I realize is me. I then jump to being on the porch and looking inside at all the light. I walk in and I'm engulfed by that light. It makes me feel weightless and peaceful. It almost lifts me off the ground. I wish I could tell you I have that feeling all the time, but I don't. I wish I could tell you it happens occasionally, but it doesn't. The fact is that it happens rarely, but when it does I *know* everything is going to be all right . . . no matter what happens.

So you're saying, "Is that it? Having a *real* relationship with God is being surrounded by light? What in the world does that mean? How does a person have a relationship with an entity that can't be seen or touched?" I can only answer for me, but this image is one of the main ways I feel a closeness or the presence of God. I think imagery can be an important piece of having a relationship with God. As humans, we want to be able to see and touch, so it's hard to put the "relate" in relationship if we can't do that. We can't put our arms around the Creator of the universe.

Since it's difficult to wrap your head around the size and scope of God, it begs the question: What do we do to have a relationship with Him? I try to do the things I would do in other relationships. I have conversations with God where I talk like I would to a friend. Now, this friend is omni-everything, and not like anyone I know, but it helps me not to always say a formal prayer. I go to Him with thoughts, wants, needs, problems, thanks, and gratitude. I've yelled, cried, laughed, and even gone through the motions when I didn't really feel like it.

I sometimes have a similar feeling that I'd describe as a "warming of the heart" that Wesley talked about. I believe that God is with me all the time, but I now make more of an effort to recognize it. I have to allow myself to feel it sometimes.

I think I've spent too much time trying to "do" something, or make it happen, making the relationship too one-sided. I pray; I talk; I cry; I reach; I, I, I, me, me, me! I now try to be more open to *receive* God, for lack of a better word. The truth is that He is here all the time, and I just have to let Him in more by relaxing, slowing down, and allowing it to happen.

It is difficult for many of us to slow down and quiet our minds enough to recognize God all around us. I feel bad saying it, but I have to work at this most of the time. I find myself searching for opportunities or moments to nurture that relationship. That moment could be church, but it's not my favorite. My favorite is when I'm alone in nature. It might also be when I'm alone in my car, or even on the lawnmower. Sometimes I can create the moment, but it's better if it just happens. I'm constantly working on recognizing those moments more so I can take advantage of them. It's so easy to fall into the everyday grind of life and forget the awesomeness of God and that He loves me and wants us to be close.

Remember the responsibility I mentioned when I walked inside? Now that I feel more of a relationship with God, I also feel more accountability. I think that's natural in relationships that are important to us. I give my parents a lot of credit for raising me to want to be a "good" person and try to do the "right" things in life. The difference now is a deeper commitment on my part. There is more introspection now. Am I doing the things that make me a better man, husband, father, friend, Christian? I know I fail at it all the time, but I'm quicker to recognize it, and I want to do better.

I hope I haven't made relating to Omni-everything sound easy. Maybe it is for some people, but not me. I'd be lying if I said it doesn't feel ridiculous sometimes. I'll be in the middle of a prayer and have this overwhelming thought that literally shouts, *This is stupid! What are you doing? You're talking to no one!* I'll regroup and try to block those thoughts out. Whenever that happens, I'm reminded of C. S. Lewis's *The Screwtape Letters*. If you haven't read the book (and you should), Screwtape is one of Satan's right-hand men and is training his nephew Wormwood as a Junior Tempter. One of the most fascinating things about the book is that it's told from Screwtape's point of view, which means that God is the enemy. It's a poignant and interesting look at all the ways we can be influenced by negative forces, even when we're trying to do the right thing. In one letter, Screwtape notices that Wormwood's "patient" continues to follow the Enemy (God) and has the audacity to be humble about it. He writes to Wormwood, "Your patient has become humble; have you drawn his attention to the fact? All virtues are less formidable to us once the man is aware that he has them, but this is specially true of humility."[*]

I do believe there is an adversary, and he wants to do everything he can to keep me from

---

[*] C. S. Lewis, *The Complete C. S. Lewis Signature Classics* (New York: HarperCollins, 2002), 224.

getting closer to God. Being inside makes me feel like I'm not in this thing alone. I need Him, and as much as other religions or practices may tell us otherwise, I realize I cannot do it on my own.

5

My Own Walk to Emmaus

After leaving the porch and going inside, I began to search for more opportunities and ways to spend time with God. The pace of modern life doesn't leave much of a chance to get away or "shut down" for any period of time. By now I had been on interferon for seven months and was giving myself shots.

During that year of treatments in 2007, my boss suggested I look at participating in a spiritual renewal weekend called Walk to Emmaus. It was a seventy-two-hour getaway from daily life, and as they say, "an opportunity to get to know Jesus in a different way." In Middle Tennessee, the Walk is hosted at my church. It has the space and facilities to host fifty men for three days. That meant I would be spending three days and nights—Thursday night through late afternoon on Sunday—with about fifty other men with no phones, computers, clocks, news, or any other contact with the outside world. And it was in the middle of football season!

I called my father in Florida and asked him if he would go with me. He had heard a little about it, and we both reluctantly decided to do it. Nobody who had ever been on the weekend would say much about what happens, so Dad and I were convinced we were going to be indoctrinated into some kind of cult. The truth is that the weekend is much more impactful if you don't know what's going to happen, so most former participants don't say much about it.

The Walk to Emmaus has been called the Protestant version of the Catholic Cursillo Movement that started in the 1960s and '70s. I highly recommend participating in these "renewal weekends," but I don't want to give any of the highlights away. For me, the Walk was a wonderful opportunity to unplug from the world and focus completely on God. There were several moments during the weekend that I experienced Him like I never had before. For three days, fifty men talked, sang, laughed, cried, learned, and got to experience the "real stuff." It was extraordinary, because maybe you've heard . . . men don't always share, sing, laugh, and cry with other men—or anyone, for that matter.

Remember earlier when I described the wave of emotion that overcame me when I was visiting my mother's church? In that instance, I felt like I needed to compose myself. After our first day on the Walk, I no longer felt the need to be composed or hold anything in at all. There was a free and uninhibited feeling that was common over that weekend, and no one seemed to feel odd about it. I remember looking over at my father during one of the songs we sang every day, and he looked like he was singing with the Metropolitan Opera! (Full disclosure—I do have a distant cousin who once sang with the Met Opera back in the day, but that gene died off quickly in the family.) As I watched him with his chest puffed out and head held high, one of those "real stuff" moments came over me. My entire body became warm and I couldn't stop smiling. I wish I could put that feeling in a bottle. I noticed I was singing at the top of my lungs as well—and never thought a moment about what it sounded like. It's an understatement to say my father and I are not good singers, but we sang every song with an abandon like never before—or since.

There was a great deal of interaction with the whole group and we were a part of several different small groups, but also had time for just the two of us. Here's the thing, though: it wasn't just the two of us. God was there . . . I was sure of it. We had the rare opportunity—particularly as men— to expose all our raw feelings and experience God's presence like we never had before.

Now, I know God is supposed to be with us all the time, but I don't *feel* it all the time. In fact, I feel it rarely. I've decided that most of that is my fault. Life is too full of distractions, and I need moments that allow me to feel His presence more. There is always going to be a reason to *not* do something when it comes to making time for ourselves and God. Stephen Covey is spot on when he says, "The key is not to prioritize what's on your schedule, but to schedule your priorities."* I need a flashing, neon sign with that written on it.

I'm always jealous of people who say they know God was talking to them, or they knew He was present at a specific time. I rarely have those feelings, or I just won't allow myself to recognize them. However, I had a particularly vivid God moment on the second night of the weekend.

I knew of a bathroom that not all the "pilgrims" knew about. It was right off the lobby of the church, and on the second night, I went to brush my teeth there before we went to bed so I didn't have to stand in line. I knew what was awaiting me back in the room and wasn't in a hurry to return. We slept on air mattresses, six to eight men to a room, and the snoring was brutal! Thankfully, we ate like kings and had more than thirty volunteers who worked to make sure we were taken care of.

---

* Steven Covey, *The 7 Habits of Highly Effective People* (New York: Free Press, 1989), 161.

I took a shortcut through the sanctuary on my way back and noticed it was completely dark in there except for a backlight on a huge cross that hung behind the altar. There was an octagonal, stained glass window glowing with lots of reds and blues above the cross, and the moonlight shining through those colors was breathtaking. It was so moving that I slowed my pace and decided to sit down on the front row, just staring at the cross and the window right above it. I sat there for several minutes, taking it all in. There were no sounds that I remember, and the temperature seemed perfect.

One moment I was enjoying the silence, and in another moment, a wave of something came over my body that I can't quite describe other than complete peace. I didn't hear any voice, but I can tell you that something very special was going on right then in that sanctuary. I was in my gym shorts, T-shirt, and holding my toothbrush and toothpaste. I really felt like I should have been dressed better . . . at least had underwear on. I guess God really does meet you wherever you are. I believe God wanted me to know that He was right there with me. I believe He is with us all the time, but we rarely recognize it or experience it. There was no question in my mind He was there. Now, *that* is real stuff.

If you're anything like me, then you need to put yourself in situations where you can think or focus on the "real stuff." At this point, you may be asking, "What exactly is the real stuff?" If you're getting out your highlighter to mark these next few sentences, go ahead and put it down. I'm not sure I have an adequate way to describe or define it. It's probably different for everyone. I can't force it to happen, but I *can* tell you that I know when it's happening. For me, it's like a different level of feeling or how I experience what's happening around me.

Now, I'm semi-famous among friends and family for getting emotional during a sweet television commercial, spending time with my family, spooning with my dog, and watching most Pixar movies. That is *not* what I'm talking about. This is a significant feeling deep in my gut, and I know God is present. I can't tell you how I know, but things seem to come together spiritually and physically for me at certain times, meaning I experience a physical sensation to accompany a spiritual moment. Maybe it's a special moment when all my family is together. Maybe it's how I look at nature when I'm able to slow down, appreciate it, and interact with it. Now that I recognize this more often, I find myself searching for more of these opportunities to talk with God, and thank Him for my life.

6

Keep on Keeping On

I love the phrase "Keep on keeping on." I remember my dad saying it some, and I've used it often over the years. Curtis Mayfield wrote a song by the same title in the early 1970s, and I found some references to the phrase as early as the 1910s. Most people seem to use it when they talk about being persistent toward a goal or destination.

I turned fifty while I was writing this. (Please pause for Darth Vader theme.) Actually, it was no big deal. The number fifty seems old to me, but I don't feel that way. I do, however, think fifty has started to *push* me. Maybe it's cancer, or maybe it's some kind of midlife crisis—although it doesn't feel like a crisis, and I haven't considered buying a new Corvette. I did, however, jump out of an airplane, mainly because I've become afraid of heights as I've gotten older. I needed to do something I was really afraid to do. My oldest daughter had done it the year before, and she convinced me I would love it. I'm not sure *love* is the word I would use, but it was an awesome experience!

I now feel this constant prodding toward making a positive impact on the world. I've accepted the responsibility of being "inside" now. I no longer find comfort in the comfort of my porch. The hard part is trying to figure out what I'm supposed to be doing with my life and how I'm supposed to impact others and the world. I feel that way more and more as I get older.

It can be overwhelming to think about making a difference in the world. What does that even mean? Well, that's the $1,000,000 question, isn't it? I feel sure I'm not alone in this thinking. We want to impact the greatest number of people possible, but what does that look like and how do we start? We also would like for it to happen in the next thirty days. We feel like we're not making a difference if it's not on some grand scale. But to be honest, I'm not sure I'll ever feel like I'm doing *enough*.

If you've ventured down this road at all, you've had someone tell you that making a difference in your own sphere of influence is just as important as some evangelist speaking in front of fifty thousand people. That may be true, but my first thought is always *go big*. I have no theological training and have never spoken in front of more than one thousand people—yet I'm sure that Rick Warren is going to ask me to fill in for him at some event at the Cowboys' stadium.

I've decided while I wait on that invitation, I should continue to work in the areas I know I have some influence. I've been involved in Big Brothers Big Sisters for several years. In late 2009, I filled out an application, had a background check, and waited to see if I would be matched with someone. I was matched with David when he was nine years old. He's now sixteen and six foot two, so it's difficult to call him a "little" brother. Anna is fifteen and Bailey is eighteen, and David fits right in with my family. I hope and pray I have been a positive influence on him as we go through life together.

Honestly, he and his mother, Tahisha, have added a dimension to my family life that we never would have had. She tells me God put me in their lives, and I feel the same about them.

Tahisha had her family in from Chicago a few Thanksgivings ago, and they invited me to come by to eat and meet everyone. Now, I am a white, blonde-headed, blue-eyed man from the South, and David and his family are all black. Most of them knew we were in the Big Brothers program, but not everyone. We had a wonderful time getting to know each other, and David confirmed later there was more than one question that went something like "What's up with the white boy who came to dinner?" I love that!

I always introduce him as my "little brother," and sometimes leave the Big Brothers thing out just to see that odd look on people's faces. The relationship is not always easy, though. Sometimes I have to straddle the line between handling things like a Big Brother and like a father. That line gets blurred sometimes, but I am thankful

for Tahisha's trust in me to handle things the best way I know how.

I have two daughters, so having a young man to mentor is different. Obviously, it's different from a racial perspective as well. Just as I try to view things as my daughters would; I try to view things from a young black man's perspective. (Don't laugh too hard; I know it's impossible, but I still try.)

I'll never forget trying to explain to David when he was much younger why his friends told him he couldn't be Batman for Halloween because Batman is white. Frankly, I wanted to punch the other kids and their parents. People suck sometimes. I tried my best to explain how some kids' upbringing allowed for ignorance. But that one wasn't in any of the Big Brother materials they gave me. His mom and I both took a stab at it. She was great, and I appreciate him indulging my feeble attempt to help. David and his family are a blessing to the Vernons, and I am grateful and honored to be his "Big Brother."

Three years ago, my Sunday school class needed to fill a spot for one of our lesson leaders. By this point, I'd gone on inside and left the comforts of the front porch. Though I still felt completely unqualified, I had substituted a couple of times and was encouraged to volunteer. If you had told me four years ago I would be leading *anything* in a Sunday school class, I would have laughed out loud. I would wager a lot that I'm on the bottom rung of the ladder in our class when it comes to knowledge of Scripture. That fact is one of the reasons I decided to do it. I'm not afraid to talk in front of a group, but my uncertainty with Scripture worried me. Having to lead lessons makes me study more so I can feel comfortable with the subject matter. I feel like I'm contributing and learning more as I continue my walk with God. It's another way for me to stay connected.

My Sunday school class has also given us the opportunity to be involved in two great ministries in our city: Community Care Fellowship and Room in the Inn. Both of these programs serve

the homeless of Nashville, and they give us more ways to act on our faith. The relationship with these organizations was already formed years ago by our church, so all we had to do was say yes. That was one of the things we said we would do for God and others—just say yes more when there is a need.

If I think about all the needs of the world too much, it starts to get suffocating. There are so many places, people, and situations that are in need that it's easy to become frozen and unable to move—or just say yes. My wife, Beth, is the best at saying yes—for herself, *and* the rest of us in the family. Many times the girls and I have "volunteered" for things we've never heard of. I like to say I'm the voice of reason. "Honey, we can't say yes to everything, or we won't do anything very well." I usually get the "That's what you can tell all your friends in Slackerville" look and end up doing it. We may end up with scheduling conflicts, or an endless supply of whatever the latest door-to-door salesperson from a broken home/putting themselves through college is selling, but Beth gets high marks for always saying yes.

I don't write about these things to say, "Hey, look at what I'm doing!" I use them as examples of my desire to put my faith and relationship with God into action. The need to do more and experience more is strong after walking in off the porch. Our family's involvement in our church has helped guide us. It rescued us from the paralyzing feeling of how and where to serve God and others—especially when you're not sure where to start.

I have no idea what God has in store for me, so I refuse to reject any possibilities. Maybe I am supposed to end up in front of thousands of people—or not. Maybe I will start giving my testimony in public more often—or not. Maybe this written story will reach lots of people and impact their lives—or not. None of us know how things are going to go, so I'm going to keep on keeping on.

7

Not All Rainbows and Unicorns

I don't want your take away from this to be, "Aw, isn't that nice. He walked on in from the porch and everything was alright. I'm not completely sure about that whole 'porch' thing—it's kind of weird, but I think I get it. They went through all that stuff, and it seems like they may have figured some things out." I can assure you we have not—particularly me! I have it figured out the least in my family. I so want my faith to be like Beth's. I've watched her faith grow stronger and stronger over these past years. I know she has her low moments, but it's like she has an impenetrable wall around her that was erected when she was going through cancer. I don't know what her wall is made out of, but it's got to be something they used on the space shuttle. I feel like my wall is made of cardboard or clay, and it's constantly crumbling or getting knocked down. I don't know if I have a faith problem, a trust problem, or a fear problem. Maybe it's all three. Maybe it's not a problem. Maybe it's just the way I'm wired. Most of the time it feels like fear. That fear may stem from not having enough trust or faith in God, but it comes without warning and I hate it.

Fear is something I've somewhat embraced most of my life. I don't mean I like it, but it drives me many times. Most of my life I've been motivated to do well by the fear of failure. I've been fortunate to be successful in certain areas, but usually the potential for success wasn't the motivating force. I excelled in school, sports, and have managed to carve out a career in the golf business that I'm proud of. I've enjoyed whatever success may have come in every area of my life, but the fear of *not* doing well is what pushed me to do well. That sounds like a sad way to go through life, but I never thought of it that way. I consider myself to be a happy, optimistic person, but I am still motivated in that manner to a certain extent. I fear not being the best husband and father I can be, so I am driven to try to live up to some unreachable standard I set. At work, I worry about all the potential issues that can keep things from going smoothly, and I know if I address them, we will do well. I fear my cancer could come back, so I pray, work out, do yoga, and drink these smoothies in the morning that look like something I've seen in a six-month-old's diaper.

As I write this it occurs to me that fear-based motivation may not be the healthiest way to approach things. These written words are pretty much the first time they've left the confines of my brain. Hold up before you start picturing me alone in a dark room, with only the glow of a small black-and-white television watching *Matlock* reruns. The point is that fear continues to be something I deal with on a semi-regular basis.

I've faced the potential death of my wife and myself at a relatively young age. I know that statistically we're not supposed to be on this side of the dirt since we both had advanced stages of cancer. Many times my brain goes to those dark places that I wish it didn't. It's those times that I hear the voice I don't want to hear. I hear a whispery, painful kind of voice that sneaks up behind me and says, "C'mon, Jim. This is cancer we're talking about here. You don't really think you all are going to beat that do you? Thousands of people die every day from cancer. What makes you think you guys are so special?" Or "C'mon, Jim. You are supposedly an educated man. Surely you don't believe in that whole triune God thing, do you? Have you ever said that out loud and listened to how ridiculous it sounds? You're kidding, right? You can't really believe that. No one can believe that!" Then I have to breathe slowly and repeat a scripture or a particular calming saying until I get my head on straight.

I love the story in the book of Mark about the father who brings his son to Jesus to be healed. Jesus asks the man if he wants Him to heal his son, and the father says, "Yes, Lord, *if you can*." Jesus says, "If I can? Don't you believe I can?" and the father says, "I believe, Lord. Help my unbelief" (Mark 9:24). I say that *all the time*. Sometimes I've said it over and over until I fell asleep when the voice (of Fear, Satan, or the Kardashians) tries to drown me.

If you saw any of the *Matrix* trilogy movies, you may remember the "Prophet" character's (Oracle) line at the end of the third installment. Now, you may not feel a *Matrix* reference is appropriate in the same chapter as the gospel of Mark, but this is how my mind works. The movies have some loosely Christian-based themes, and I focused on them as much as I did all of the action, violence, and things blowing up. If you haven't seen them, the main character (Neo) is played by Keanu Reeves, and he sacrifices himself to save humanity. At the end of the third film, the Oracle is questioned if she knew everything was going to be alright. She replies, "Oh, no . . . I didn't know ... but I believed." Like her, I don't know how much I know, but I know how much I believe.

I've told many people that I would like for the voice of God to sound just like James Earl Jones and tell me what to do and say that everything is going to be all right. But, for whatever reason, God has decided not to communicate with me that way, so I have to look harder for His "voice." I have to pay attention more. Most of the time I have to be smacked in the face.

For example, it took me three years to pull the trigger on making that call to Big Brothers Big Sisters. Three years! My wife and mother had both repeatedly suggested some type of mentoring program to me over the years, and then they both randomly said something to me in the span of a week or so. I assumed they had spoken to each other, but they had not. I said a prayer about it, but still didn't make the call. A few days later, I was driving down the road and heard a siren nearby. I had to really strain to look over my left shoulder to see what was going on, and the first thing that caught my eye was a huge billboard advertisement recruiting for Big Brothers Big Sisters. Once again I said, "Okay, Lord, I get it."

Just because I look for His "voice" more now, it doesn't mean it's easy for me to recognize it. I believe God works through other people too, so my mind has a tendency to go a little nuts sometimes with that one. If God can communicate with us any way He wants, then I may over-interpret things I see or hear. If I have something I really need direction on, I end up wondering if the infomercial I saw at 1:00 a.m. had a message that God was trying to give me. I know it sounds crazy, but it's never dull in my head.

On the other hand, I have a friend I got to know about a year before Beth and I got cancer. Over the last nine years, he has become a major rock for me when I am feeling weak or low. I've had lots of people pray for me over the years, but this friend's prayers are different. I'm hopeful when other people pray for me, but I really believe it when he says it. He is a retired Special Forces guy with an unbelievable testimony. I don't know exactly why he impacts me that way, but I am so thankful he is in my life. I am certain God has used him to talk to me at times. I now pray for God to help me understand that I'm not supposed to understand everything. And I need to go to sleep earlier so I avoid considering buying knives at 1:00 a.m. that can cut through a boot.

I can't always tell what is coincidence and what is God in this life. Maybe there is no such thing as coincidence; I don't really know. It seems like there are lots of things I don't know when it comes to God. I've said before that once I get past the top ten items carved in the stone tablets, I have a lot of "gray" in my life. I'm constantly praying for wisdom and direction on many of the tough topics that divide the church but never seem to get an answer. I have a hard enough time rebuilding my own wall of faith that I don't have the time or inclination to judge others—or profess to know how God works. What I do know is that He loves me and wants me to be with Him. With His help, I'm going to keep working on all the other stuff.

8

Send in the Cavalry, I Need Calvary!

Unfortunately, it took cancer for me to figure out how little I really control in this world. All too often it seems that tragedies or crises are required for people to stop relying solely on themselves. In fact, much of our American culture has been founded on an independent, entrepreneurial, frontier spirit. While I love those qualities, I also believe it can hinder us from leaving our porches and going inside.

The phrase I hear most to describe this is *surrendering to God.* This can be a really big stumbling block for many people. The need to control is very strong in many of us. Even the word *surrender* has such a negative connotation; we don't like using it—or doing it. It's not easy and rarely happens with a light-switch type of event: "Okay! Now I've surrendered. Glad that's done."

There are so many distractions in modern-day life that we always seem to fall back into our routines and think we're in control again. For me, it's a continuous cycle of realization, acceptance, and surrender. I realize (again) that so much of my life is not in my control. I accept that fact. I let go of the need to control everything and allow God to work in me and through me. Wash, rinse, repeat…

As much as I hate to say it, I wonder if I would yearn for God the way I do now if it hadn't been for cancer. My world came crashing down in a matter of six months in 2006, and it became very apparent to me that I needed help—I needed both a cavalry and Calvary! Are you picturing the soldiers on horseback and hearing that familiar bugle refrain as they race toward you to help? Are you picturing Jesus on the cross at Calvary and thinking, "He did that for me?" I'm not just talking about friends and family lending their help and support. I'm talking about something bigger than what we can see and touch; something inside that lets us know there is more to life than our everyday existence on this planet. Something more significant than what our brains can fully comprehend.

I believe this, but I wonder sometimes if I believe it just because I *want* it to be so. I don't have the type of faith that asks few questions and is at peace most of the time in my mind. I question, ponder, wonder, and contemplate all things regarding my faith. Beth asks me all the time, "Why can't you just believe and move on?" I can tell she's checked that one off her list.

I'm envious of that type of faith. More than likely, I would have been like Thomas and had to put my finger in Jesus's side for proof when He appeared to the disciples after the crucifixion. I don't know if that's a good thing or a bad thing. But I often wonder if God looks at me, shaking His head, saying, "Jim, we covered this quite a while ago. Stop beating a dead horse and let's move forward." Or maybe it's more like, "Way to go, son. Keep grinding it out in your mind—everything is going to be okay." I really hope it's the latter. Needless to say, I'm a work in progress. I'm guessing you and I have that in common.

When the time comes that you need a cavalry and Calvary, don't be afraid to surrender to that need. If you have trouble with the word *surrender*, then think of it as allowing God to take control of the things you realize you can't. My mom gave me a great prayer that I use a lot: "Lord, let me rest in You while You work through me." Acknowledge what Jesus did for you and let the bugle roar!

Now What?

So here we are. Now what are we supposed to do?

I can only speak for me, but this faith, God, Trinity, trust thing is not always easy. I have to work at it. I now have regular discussions with family and friends about God and the many things we don't understand about this life and what comes next. Like many people, I have so many questions, and so few answers. I often feel like I fail miserably and fall short of what I consider mediocre faith and trust. I'm not proud to say that I have to make time to nurture my relationship with God. I've always considered that important with my family, and I make it a priority. Why isn't it that easy for me to make it a priority with God? I have no good answer other than I'm a flawed human. I *can* say that I will never stop trying to get better at it.

I'm not big on unsolicited advice, so I'm going to call this a suggestion. I've shared parts of this story enough times that I know there are others who have some of the same thoughts and feelings that I have. They stand on that porch just like I did and stare inside, wondering. They know that there is something more to their faith and relationship with God, but they can't put their finger on it.

After that first time I gave my testimony at church, a friend of mine gave me the idea of putting this on paper and told me to call it "Life on the Porch." I thought it was fitting because I spent most of my life on the porch, but this story is really about having the courage to walk on inside—to move outside what is comfortable into something more significant.

Whatever it is in your life that is keeping you from walking on inside to a more meaningful connection with God—let . . . it . . . go. It's not worth it. We all have that "stuff" or "baggage" in our lives that keeps us from doing great things. For me, cancer pushed me in the door. If you don't have anything pushing you inside, maybe there is something blocking you from getting in. Identify what that something is and work on moving it out of the way. I truly believe it will be the best step you ever take in your life.

So let it go. And walk on inside.

22473608R00048

Made in the USA
Columbia, SC
01 August 2018